Preface

Online communities have become an indispensable tool for businesses across various industries, with the blockchain sector being no exception. In this rapidly evolving landscape, networking and collaboration are crucial for success. Fostering a thriving online community, however, goes beyond merely connecting people with a common interest or goal. It requires a shared purpose that transcends the initial connection, nurturing strong relationships and encouraging engagement to establish a flourishing community.

This comprehensive guide serves as a valuable resource for those looking to develop, manage, and grow an online community within the blockchain sector. It explores the importance of community management, the role of a community manager, and the various aspects of building a strong community. We also delve into managing conflicts and disagreements, as well as identifying and addressing spammers, scammers, and other malicious actors within the community.

Furthermore, this guide provides insights on developing a community growth strategy that leverages social media, online channels, events, contests, and giveaways. It also discusses the ongoing role of community management and the importance of adapting to changing community needs and trends.

Equipped with resources and tools for community managers, as well as a glossary of community management terms, this guide aims to empower you with the knowledge and strategies needed to create and maintain a thriving, engaged, and secure community in the dynamic world of blockchain

Contents

1

The Importance of Community Management

Introduction

Over the past decade, the blockchain sector has experienced remarkable growth, leading to a surge in online communities centred around shared interests and needs. These communities span discussion forums, social media groups, messaging platforms, marketplaces, gaming platforms, and online education platforms. While some communities have thrived, others have faltered in gaining traction or maintaining their growth. **The presence of a <u>shared purpose</u> beyond the initial connection is a critical factor distinguishing successful communities from unsuccessful ones.**

Before exploring the significance of shared purpose, it is crucial to define key concepts such as *successful community*, and *shared purpose*. A successful community can be defined as one which fosters engagement, trust, and collaboration among its members, achieving its intended goals such as knowledge sharing, networking, or innovation. Shared purpose refers to a unifying goal, value, or need that motivates individuals to join and participate in a community beyond the initial connection.

The importance of community management in online communities can be observed in several key areas:

1. **Building trust and credibility**: An effectively managed community signals to its members that their opinions and contributions are valued. This fosters a sense of trust and credibility, which can encourage members to actively participate, share their insights, and provide support to their peers.

2. **Nurturing engagement and collaboration**: Community managers play a vital role in creating an environment that promotes healthy and constructive engagement between members. By facilitating discussions, organising events, and highlighting member achievements, community managers can nurture an atmosphere of collaboration and collective learning.

3. **Maintaining a safe and inclusive space**: Online communities can be vulnerable to various threats, such as spammers, scammers, and trolls. Community managers are responsible for identifying and addressing these issues, ensuring that the community remains a safe and inclusive space for all members.

4. **Guiding the community's growth and direction**: The community manager's role includes monitoring the community's goals, trends, and interests. They are instrumental in shaping the community's direction, identifying potential opportunities for growth, and implementing changes to better serve the community's needs.

5. **Retaining and attracting new members**: A well-managed community is more likely to retain its existing members and attract new ones. Community managers play a crucial role in promoting the community, highlighting its value proposition, and creating a welcoming environment for newcomers.

6. **Facilitating communication between members and stakeholders**: In many cases, online communities serve as a bridge between members and external stakeholders, such as project teams, company representatives, or

content creators. Community managers act as liaisons, ensuring that relevant information is communicated effectively and that member concerns are addressed.

The Shared Purpose Factor

In the realm of community building, there is a vital factor that serves as the cornerstone of a thriving collective—a factor that distinguishes successful communities from those that fall short. This chapter explores the significance of a central element called the "Shared Purpose Factor" in community building, highlighting its vital importance in cultivating engaged and purpose-driven communities. Understanding and harnessing the power of the Shared Purpose Factor is essential for creating spaces where individuals come together, connect, and collaborate towards a common mission.

The Shared Purpose Factor represents the deep-rooted desire within individuals to be part of something greater than themselves—a collective pursuit of a shared goal or mission. It goes beyond the superficial aspects of community building and delves into the fundamental elements that bind individuals together, fostering a sense of belonging, connection, and engagement.

By tapping into the Shared Purpose Factor, community builders can establish a strong foundation that supports the growth and vitality of their communities. It becomes the driving force that guides community members, shapes their interactions, and fuels their collective efforts towards a higher purpose. Whether it's a cause, a vision for change, or a shared interest, the Shared Purpose Factor provides the necessary framework for individuals to rally around, creating a sense of unity and common identity.

When the Shared Purpose Factor is effectively nurtured, it acts as a catalyst for meaningful engagement, collaboration, and collective impact. It anchors the community, providing stability and support, while also fostering adaptability and resilience in the face of challenges. It becomes the wellspring from which ideas, innovation, and shared wisdom flow, nourishing the community and facilitating personal and collective growth.

In this chapter, we will explore the significance of the Shared Purpose Factor in the context of community building. We will delve into how it shapes the foundation of purpose-driven communities, distinguishes them from other forms of collective spaces, and guides the essential steps involved in cultivating vibrant and impactful communities. Drawing upon the metaphor of divining water and building a well, we will uncover the crucial steps required to construct a thriving and engaging collective space. By understanding the power and importance of the Shared Purpose Factor, community builders can unlock the true potential of their communities, creating spaces where individuals find meaning, connection, and fulfilment in their collective endeavours.

We will also address the common pitfalls of building communities solely around a product or in unsuitable circumstances, emphasising the importance of authentic growth. By highlighting the significance of this authentic growth and its alignment with purpose, we can ensure that communities flourish in a meaningful and sustainable manner.

Step 1: Divining the Water - Cultivating a Concept to Rally Around
Before a well can be built, there is a process of divining the water—a search for the source of inspiration and the concept that will resonate with the community. In the context of community building, this entails cultivating a clear and compelling idea or purpose that ignites the passion and enthusiasm of potential community members. This concept becomes the driving force that unifies individuals and provides a shared mission to rally around.

Differentiation: Many communities fall into the trap of solely focusing on their product, neglecting the need for a higher purpose or connecting with the deeper aspirations of their audience. Purpose-driven communities, however, cultivate a concept that goes beyond the product or service, encompassing a vision for change or a commitment to a broader impact.

Step 2: Building the Well - Establishing the Platform and Infrastructure
Once the water has been divined and the concept solidified, the next step is to build the well—the platform and infrastructure that will support and facilitate the purpose-driven community. This entails establishing a dedicated space where community members can come together, connect, and engage in meaningful ways.

Differentiation: Many communities focus solely on building a platform without considering the underlying purpose or the necessary supportive infrastructure. Purpose-driven communities recognise the importance of aligning the platform and infrastructure with the community's values and objectives. They prioritise creating a safe and inclusive environment, providing resources and mentorship programmes, and designing engaging spaces for meaningful interactions.

Step 3: Drawing from the Wellspring - Encouraging Active Engagement
A well's value lies in people drawing from its life-giving waters. Similarly, a thriving community relies on active participation and engagement from its members. By fostering an environment that encourages individuals to contribute their thoughts, ideas, and expertise, the community draws from the collective knowledge and experiences of its members. This active participation breathes life into the community, creating a dynamic and enriching space for all involved.

Differentiation: Many communities struggle to foster active engagement, resulting in passive audiences and limited interactions. Purpose-driven communities prioritise meaningful engagement, encouraging members to actively contribute their knowledge, experiences, and perspectives. They create opportunities for collaboration, learning, and growth, making the community a vibrant and interactive space.

Step 4: Nurturing the Wellspring - Providing Support and Resources

Just as a well requires maintenance and care to ensure a continuous supply of clean water, a thriving community requires ongoing support and resources. This includes providing guidance, resources, and mentorship to community members. It also involves nurturing a culture of support and collaboration, where members can seek assistance, share knowledge, and grow together.

Differentiation: Many communities fail to provide adequate support and resources to their members, resulting in a lack of growth and engagement. Purpose-driven communities prioritise the continuous nurturing of the community, offering guidance, resources, and mentorship programmes. They foster a culture of support, collaboration, and continuous learning, ensuring the wellspring of the community remains vibrant and sustainable.

Conclusion:
In conclusion, the process of building a purpose-driven community parallels the journey of divining the water and constructing the well. By cultivating a concept to rally around, building a platform and infrastructure, encouraging active engagement, and providing support and resources, a purpose-driven community can flourish authentically. This approach stands in contrast to communities built solely around a product or those formed in unsuitable circumstances, as purpose-driven communities prioritise a higher mission, create meaningful engagement, and offer ongoing support. By understanding these differences and embracing purpose-driven community building, we can lay the foundation for constructing communities that enrich the lives of their members and make a lasting positive impact.

<u>Spotlight on Successful Online Communities</u>

In this chapter, we will explore how successful online communities have harnessed the power of shared purpose to create engaging, collaborative, and resilient spaces for their members, while also acknowledging some of the challenges they face. We will delve into real-world examples, examining how these communities have leveraged a strong sense of purpose to foster deep connections, drive innovation, and contribute to the growth and success of their respective ecosystems. We will also examine a cautionary tale of a community built without a shared purpose, highlighting the importance of a well-defined vision in community building.

Case Study 1: Ethereum - Decentralising the Internet

Ethereum, a decentralised platform for building and deploying smart contracts and decentralised applications, has cultivated a thriving community focused on creating a more open, decentralised, and accessible internet. The Ethereum community collaborates on protocol improvements, research, and development of decentralised applications, all contributing to the growth and success of the Ethereum ecosystem. This sense of purpose has led to the establishment of a vibrant community that fosters innovation and supports the development of numerous projects.

However, Ethereum has also faced challenges, such as network congestion, high transaction fees, and scalability issues. Some members may become frustrated with these limitations, leading to disagreements within the community. Despite these challenges, the shared purpose has kept the community focused on finding solutions and improving the platform.

Key Takeaway: A clear vision and sense of purpose can unite community members, guiding their efforts to contribute and collaborate effectively, even in the face of challenges.

Case Study 2: Gitcoin - Sustaining and Growing the Open-Source Ecosystem

Gitcoin is a platform that connects developers with open-source projects in need of funding and support. The community's focus on sustaining and growing the open-source ecosystem has led to active participation in grant rounds, provision of feedback on projects, and sharing resources to support developers. As a result, the Gitcoin community has nurtured numerous open-source projects, leading to the development of innovative solutions in the blockchain space and fostering a strong sense of camaraderie and mutual support among its members.

However, the nature of open-source projects can sometimes lead to disagreements over project direction, funding allocation, and intellectual property rights. While these conflicts can create tension within the community, the shared purpose of sustaining and growing the open-source ecosystem helps maintain overall cohesion and collaboration.

Key Takeaway: By rallying around a shared objective, community members can create deep connections and a sense of camaraderie that can weather challenges and changes.

Case Study 3: Giveth - Revolutionising Philanthropy

Giveth is a decentralised platform focused on creating a more transparent and accountable charitable giving system. The community's commitment to revolutionising the philanthropic sector is evident in the development of tools and processes that facilitate direct giving and ensure transparency. This shared purpose leads to deeper connections as community members collaborate to create solutions that address social and environmental issues while maintaining trust and accountability.

Nonetheless, Giveth faces challenges in the form of scepticism about the effectiveness of decentralised philanthropy, regulatory hurdles, and competition from traditional charitable organisations. These challenges can strain the community's unity, but the shared purpose of revolutionising philanthropy keeps members focused on their common goal.

Key Takeaway: A shared purpose that aligns with the values and goals of the community members can foster emotional investment and long-term commitment, even when confronted with obstacles.

Case Study 4: Fyre Festival - A Cautionary Tale of Community Building Gone Wrong

Fyre Festival, a luxury music festival promoted by entrepreneur Billy McFarland and rapper Ja Rule, stands as a cautionary tale of how attempting to create a community without a shared purpose can lead to spectacular failure. Marketed as an exclusive, high-end event, Fyre Festival attracted attendees with the promise of luxury accommodations, gourmet food, and A-list music performances on a private island in the Bahamas.

However, the event organisers failed to deliver on their promises. Instead of a well-planned, high-quality experience, attendees arrived to find a chaotic, disorganised event with inadequate infrastructure, food, and accommodations. The festival was quickly cancelled, and the organisers faced numerous lawsuits and criminal charges.

Fyre Festival's failure can be attributed to its lack of a shared purpose. The event was primarily driven by marketing hype and the pursuit of short-term profits, rather than a genuine commitment to creating a unique and memorable experience for its community. The lack of a unifying vision and purpose led to poor planning, mismanagement, and ultimately, the event's disastrous outcome.

Key Takeaway: A community built solely on hype and superficial attractions, without a well-defined shared purpose, is more likely to collapse under pressure and fail to deliver meaningful, lasting value to its members.

The Role of a Community Manager

A community ambassador is responsible for not only overseeing and nurturing their own online community but also representing their project or company in other forums and groups. This role combines community management and marketing efforts to build a strong, positive image for the project or company both internally and externally. The community ambassador plays a multifaceted role that includes the following key responsibilities:

1. **Developing and implementing community guidelines**: Establishing clear rules and expectations for member behaviour is essential for maintaining a respectful and inclusive environment. Community ambassadors are responsible for creating these guidelines and ensuring that they are enforced consistently and fairly within their community.
2. **Moderating content and discussions**: Community ambassadors monitor and review content posted by members, intervening when necessary to address inappropriate behaviour, resolve disputes, or guide discussions in a productive direction.
3. **Fostering engagement**: Encouraging active participation and interaction among members is a primary goal of community ambassadors. They can achieve this by initiating discussions, sharing relevant content, and creating opportunities for members to connect with one another.

4. **Managing and mentoring moderators**: A community ambassador may work with a team of moderators to help maintain order and uphold community standards. This involves providing guidance, support, and training to ensure that moderation efforts are consistent and effective.
5. **Representing the community's interests**: As the liaison between community members and the organisation or project leaders, a community ambassador must effectively communicate member concerns, feedback, and suggestions to the appropriate parties.
6. **Joining and participating in external forums and groups**: Community ambassadors play a crucial role in spreading awareness about their project or company by actively participating in other forums and groups relevant to their demographic. This involves engaging in meaningful discussions, answering questions, and sharing valuable insights, without resorting to aggressive promotion or "shilling."
7. **Building relationships with external communities**: As representatives of their project or company, community ambassadors should focus on establishing and maintaining positive relationships with other communities, influencers, and thought leaders in their industry. This helps to build a strong network of support and collaboration, which can lead to potential partnerships and opportunities.
8. **Tracking and analysing community metrics**: Community ambassadors are responsible for monitoring and assessing the health of the community through key performance indicators (KPIs) such as

engagement levels, member retention, and growth. This data can inform strategic decisions and help identify areas for improvement.

9. **Promoting and growing the community**: To ensure the ongoing success and sustainability of the community, ambassadors must actively promote it and attract new members. This may involve leveraging social media, partnerships, and other marketing channels to raise awareness and drive growth.

Summary

Effective community management is indispensable, as it facilitates the establishment of trust and credibility, fosters engagement and collaboration, ensures a safe and inclusive environment, directs the community's growth and trajectory, retains and recruits new members, and enhances communication between members and stakeholders.

The significance of shared purpose is exemplified through various successful online communities in the blockchain sector, such as Ethereum, Gitcoin, and Giveth. These communities coalesce around mutual goals, values, and interests, which contribute to their overall success.

Community ambassadors occupy a central role in the administration and nurturing of these online communities. Their multifaceted responsibilities encompass the development and implementation of community guidelines, moderation of content and discussions, cultivation of engagement, management and mentorship of moderators, representation of the community's interests, participation in external forums and groups, relationship-building with external communities, monitoring and analysis of community metrics, and promotion and growth of the community. By fulfilling these duties, community ambassadors substantially contribute to the evolution of robust, successful, and purpose-driven communities within the blockchain sector.

2

Building a strong Community

Group Types - _Open vs Closed Groups_

Open Groups:

Open groups are communities on platforms like Telegram and Discord where anyone can join and participate. These groups have no restrictions on language, topics, or behaviour, and often follow a free-for-all style of moderation. Anyone can send messages, images, and files, and there are no filters or barriers to entry.

Pros of Open Groups:

1. **Accessibility**: _Anyone can join an open group, making it easy to find and connect with people who share similar interests._
2. **Free expression**: _Open groups allow for uncensored expression and the sharing of ideas without fear of censorship or retribution._
3. **Large user base**: _Since open groups have no restrictions, they can attract a large number of users and have more diverse discussions._
4. **No moderators**: _Open groups require no active moderation, which can save time and resources._
5. **Open debate**: _Discussions in open groups can be more heated and passionate, leading to a more engaging and stimulating environment._
6. **No restrictions on language**: _Open groups have no restrictions on the use of certain words or phrases, which can foster an atmosphere of open communication._
7. **Anonymity**: _Open groups can allow for anonymous participation, which can enable people to express themselves more freely._

8. **No censorship**: *Open groups are not subject to censorship, allowing for the free exchange of information and ideas.*

Cons of Open Groups:

1. **Trolls**: *Open groups are more susceptible to trolling and disruptive behaviour, which can degrade the quality of the discussion.*
2. **Off-topic discussions**: *Since there are no restrictions on the topics discussed, open groups can easily veer off-topic, making it difficult to stay focused on the original subject.*
3. **Inappropriate content**: *Without moderation, open groups can be a breeding ground for inappropriate or offensive content.*
4. **No control**: *Since there are no moderators, there is no control over the direction of the discussion or the behaviour of the users.*
5. **Harassment**: *Open groups can be a hotbed for harassment and bullying, which can make some users feel uncomfortable or unsafe.*
6. **Lack of organisation**: *Without any structure or rules, open groups can be chaotic and difficult to navigate.*
7. **Lower quality discussions**: *With no restrictions or rules, discussions in open groups can often be low quality or lack substance.*
8. **No filter**: *Open groups have no filter for spam or unwanted content, which can clutter the discussion and make it hard to find useful information.*

Closed Groups:

closed groups are communities that have certain restrictions on language, topics, and behaviour. These groups have moderators who ensure that the community guidelines are followed and that discussions remain on-topic and respectful.

Pros of Closed Groups:

1. **Quality discussions**: *closed groups tend to have higher quality discussions, as moderators ensure that participants stay on-topic and contribute meaningful content.*
2. **Safe environment**: *closed groups provide a safe environment where users can express their opinions without fear of harassment or bullying.*
3. **Professionalism**: *closed groups often have a more professional atmosphere, which can be appealing for networking and business purposes.*
4. **Active moderation**: *Moderators can actively control the direction of the discussion and maintain a level of quality in the content shared.*
5. **Higher engagement**: *closed groups can foster higher levels of engagement, as participants are more likely to contribute constructively when guidelines are enforced.*
6. **Community guidelines**: *closed groups typically have clear guidelines that establish expectations for behaviour and content, making it easier to know what is appropriate and what is not.*

7. ***No unwanted content***: *closed groups have filters for spam and unwanted content, which keeps the discussion focused and useful.*
8. ***Community growth***: *closed groups can foster a sense of community and encourage growth as users are more likely to stay engaged and participate over time.*

Cons of closed Groups:

1. **Restricted expression**: *closed groups may have restrictions on language, topics, and behaviour, which can limit free expression and creativity.*
2. **Gatekeeping**: *closed groups may have strict membership requirements or an application process, making it harder for new users to join.*
3. **Slow moderation**: *closed groups may have slower response times for moderation, which can result in delayed discussions or unresolved conflicts.*
4. **Potential bias**: *Moderators may have biases or personal opinions that influence their decisions, which can lead to unfair treatment of certain users or topics.*
5. **Limited debate**: *closed groups may limit debate or discussion on certain topics, which can stifle dissenting opinions or alternative viewpoints.*
6. **Time-consuming**: *closed groups require active moderation, which can be time-consuming and require a dedicated team or individual.*
7. **Censorship**: *closed groups may engage in censorship, which can prevent the free exchange of information and ideas.*
8. **Less anonymity:** *closed groups may require users to use standard names, which can compromise anonymity and privacy.*

Open/closed Summary

Open and closed groups have their respective advantages and disadvantages. Open groups are more accessible and allow for uncensored expression, while closed groups provide a safe environment with higher-quality discussions.

When deciding which type of group is most suited to a project, several factors should be considered, such as the project's purpose, the target audience, and the desired level of engagement and moderation. For example, if the project aims to foster open debate and free expression, an open group may be more appropriate. On the other hand, if the project focuses on professional networking or requires a more structured environment, a closed group may be better suited.

Ultimately, the decision to use an open or closed group will depend on the goals and values of the project, as well as the preferences of the target audience. It's important to weigh the pros and cons of each type of group carefully and choose the option that best aligns with the project's objectives.

Setting Community Guidelines

Community guidelines provide the foundation for a well-functioning online community, setting clear expectations for member behaviour and interaction. These guidelines help maintain a respectful and inclusive atmosphere, while also providing a framework for addressing conflicts and violations. To create effective community guidelines, consider the following steps:

1. **Define the purpose and values of your community**: Begin by outlining the core objectives and values of your community. This will help shape the specific rules and expectations you establish. For example, if your community prioritises collaboration and support, emphasise the importance of constructive feedback and open communication in your guidelines.

2. **Establish clear rules for conduct**: Clearly outline the expected behaviour of community members. Include specifics on what is considered acceptable and unacceptable, such as prohibitions on hate speech, discrimination, harassment, or sharing explicit content. Provide examples when possible to help members understand the nuances of each rule.

3. **Address user-generated content**: Clearly state your policies regarding the sharing of external links, promotional content, and user-generated content. Specify the types of content that are allowed and those that are prohibited. Additionally, outline any attribution or copyright requirements for sharing content created by others.

4. **Highlight the importance of privacy and personal information**: Encourage members to protect their personal information and respect the privacy of others. Discourage the sharing of sensitive data, such as phone numbers, email addresses, or personal photographs, without explicit consent. Include guidelines on how to handle instances where a user's privacy has been compromised.

5. **Specify consequences for violating guidelines**: Clearly outline the potential consequences for violating community guidelines, such as warnings, temporary suspensions, or permanent bans. Establish a fair and consistent process for addressing violations, and communicate this process to your members.

6. **Outline procedures for reporting and addressing violations**: Provide clear instructions on how community members can report violations or conflicts to moderators or administrators. Explain the steps that will be taken to investigate and address reported issues, and ensure that members are aware of their rights and responsibilities when it comes to addressing violations.

7. **Encourage positive behaviour and contributions**: In addition to outlining prohibited behaviours, emphasise the positive actions and attitudes you want to foster within your community. This may include guidelines for providing constructive criticism, offering support, or sharing relevant resources.

8. **Review and update guidelines regularly:** As your community evolves, it is essential to revisit and update your guidelines to address new issues, clarify ambiguities, or refine rules. Encourage community members to provide feedback on the guidelines and participate in discussions about potential changes.

By creating comprehensive, specific, and actionable community guidelines, you can establish a strong foundation for your online community. These guidelines will help members understand the expectations for behaviour, ensure a safe and inclusive environment, and provide a clear framework for addressing conflicts and violations.

Setting up a basic Telegram group

Setup

PC - 5 step

Step 1: Open the Telegram application on your PC.
To create a new group on Telegram from your PC, open the Telegram application on your computer.

Step 2: Click on the three horizontal lines icon located at the top left corner of the screen.

Click on the three horizontal lines icon at the top left corner of the screen to access the drop-down menu.

Step 3: Select "New Group" from the drop-down menu.
From the drop-down menu, select "New Group" to create a new group.

Step 4: Input the desired name for your group in the pop-up box.
In the pop-up box that appears, input the desired name for your group.

Step 5: Add at least one member to the group.
To proceed with creating your group, add at least one member to the group. You can do this by typing their username into the search bar and selecting the correct profile from the drop-down list.

Mobile (ios) - 6 step

Step 1: Open the Telegram app on your iOS device.

To create a new group on Telegram on iOS, open the Telegram app on your iOS device.

Step 2: Tap the pencil icon in the bottom right corner of the screen.

Tap the pencil icon in the bottom right corner of the screen to create a new message.

Step 3: Select "New Group" from the list of options.

From the list of options, select "New Group" to create a new group.

Step 4: Choose at least one member to add to the group.

Choose at least one member to add to the group by selecting their name from your contact list.

Step 5: Input the desired name for your group.

Input the desired name for your group in the provided text field.

Step 6: Tap "Create" to create your new group.

Tap "Create" to finalise the creation of your new group on iOS.

Mobile (Android) - 6 steps

Step 1: Open the Telegram app on your Android device.
To create a new group on Telegram on Android, open the Telegram app on your Android device.

Step 2: Tap the floating action button in the bottom right corner of the screen.
Tap the floating action button in the bottom right corner of the screen to create a new message.

Step 3: Select "New Group" from the list of options.
From the list of options, select "New Group" to create a new group.

Step 4: Choose at least one member to add to the group.
Choose at least one member to add to the group by selecting their name from your contact list.

Step 5: Input the desired name for your group.
Input the desired name for your group in the provided text field.

Step 6: Tap "Create" to create your new group.
Tap "Create" to finalise the creation of your new group on Android.

Basic Settings (PC)

(Profile picture, group name, chat history)

Navigate to your group page and click on the three vertical dots located in the top right corner.

To customise your group's basic settings from your PC, navigate to your group page and click on the three vertical dots located in the top right corner.

Select "Manage Group" from the drop-down menu.

From the drop-down menu that appears, select "Manage Group" to access the basic settings of your group.

Add a profile picture to your group.

To add a profile picture to your group, click on the camera icon and choose a picture from your device to upload.

Set or change the display name of the group.

To set or change the display name of the group, click on the current group name. A text field will appear where you can input the new display name.

Change the group type to public.

Select the option from the list to change the group type to public.

Ensure the group name is unique.

Make sure the group name is unique, as Telegram does not allow duplicate names.

Enable viewing of chat history for members.

To enable viewing of chat history for members, toggle the option in the settings.

Customise the Bot

Disclaimer: The instructions provided herein utilise the functionalities of Telegram's BotFather and GroupHelpBot as examples. Their use is illustrative and does not indicate endorsement of these specific bots by the author or any associated party. Other bots may be used to achieve similar results. As with any online tool, users should research and choose bots and services according to their needs and the credibility of the bot developer. Always be wary of sharing sensitive information with bots and consider the privacy and security implications of their use.

Access BotFather in Telegram.

To customise your bot, you need to access BotFather in Telegram. This involves opening the Telegram application and typing '@BotFather' in the search bar. Select the correct profile from the search results.

Create your new bot.

In the BotFather's chat, type '/newbot' and follow the instructions given to create your new bot. You will need to provide a display name and a username for your new bot.

Set the profile picture for your bot.

After creating your bot, type '/setuserpic' in the BotFather's chat. From the drop-down list, select the new bot that you just created, and then send the picture you want to use as your custom bot's image to BotFather.

Forward the token message to '@GroupHelpBot'.
After setting up your bot's profile picture, forward the token message that BotFather gives you to the bot '@GroupHelpBot'. This will allow your custom bot to access the necessary permissions to be added to your group and perform its functions.

.

Custom Bot Commands for Group Help

1. Bot Reload & User Management

    a. Use these commands to manage users in your group:
        i. **/reload**: *Reload the bot*
        ii. **/ban, /multiban, /mban**: *Ban one or more users*
        iii. **/kick, /multikick, /mkick**: *Kick one or more users*
        iv. **/warn, /warns**: *Warn a user or manage/view user warnings*
        v. **/mute, /multimute, /mmute**: *Mute one or more users*
        vi. **/unban, /multiunban, /munban**: *Unban one or more users*
        vii. **/unwarn**: *Remove a user's warning*
        viii. **/unmute, /multiunmute, /munmute**: *Unmute one or more users*
        ix. **/info, /infopvt**: *Get information about a user or get user information in private chat*

2. Message & Content Management

a. These commands help you manage messages and content:

    i. **/del, /delall, /multidel, /mdel, /purge**: *Delete a user's message, delete all messages from a certain point, or delete a range of messages*

    ii. **/delban, /delkick, /delwarn, /delmute**: *Ban, kick, warn, or mute a user and delete their message*

3. Content & Command Customization

  a. Utilise these commands to create personalised commands and adjust content settings:

    i. **/personal**: *Create a new personal command*

    ii. **/remove**: *Remove a personal command*

    iii. **/reply**: *Create a new personal reply*

    iv. **/unreply**: *Remove a personal reply*

    v. **/antiflood**: *Customise the anti flood*

4. User & Group Information

  a. Use these commands to access information about users and your group:

    i. **/listroles**: *Send the user's roles list in private chat*

    ii. **/list**: *Send the list of all the users in your group in private chat*

    iii. **/inactives**: *Send the list of all the inactive users in your group in private chat*

    iv. **/chatid**: *Get the chat_id of your group*

5. 6.5 Message Control & Pin Management

a. These commands allow you to manage messages and pin content within the group:
    i. **/send**: *Send a message using the bot itself, in your group*
    ii. **/pin**: *Send a message and pin it in the group*
    iii. **/npin**: *Send a message from the Bot and pin it with notification*
    iv. **/spin**: *Send a message from the Bot and pin it without notification*
    v. **/editpin**: *Edit the pinned message*
    vi. **/delpin**: *Delete the pinned message*
    vii. **/repin**: *Remove the pinned message and re-send it in the group*
    viii. **/unpinall**: *Removes all pinned messages*

6. Command, Role & Content Management

    a. These commands help you manage roles, commands, and content:
        i. **/commands**: *List of all the personal commands*
        ii. **/ammoniti**: *List of the warned user*
        iii. **/block**: *Block a gif or a sticker*
        iv. **/unblock**: *Unblock the gif or the sticker*
        v. **/magic**: *Transform a gif or a sticker into a command*
        vi. **/unmagic**: *Remove the association of a gif or sticker from a command*
        vii. **/geturl**: *Get the URL of a message*

7. User Engagement & Analytics

    a. These commands provide insights into user engagement and offer interactive features:

i. **/graphic**: *Trend of the number of subs in your group (graphic)*
ii. **/trend**: *Trend of the number of subs in your group (message)*
iii. **/views**: *View active users*
iv. **/top10**: *Show the 10 most active*

Community manager internal guidelines

1.   Don't make assumptions: It's essential to remain open-minded and curious about the needs and preferences of your community members. Actively listen (as opposed to passively) to their concerns and ideas, and engage in conversations to deepen your understanding. This approach will enable you to identify and address the community's genuine needs and avoid implementing solutions that may not resonate with its members.

2.   Beware of quick fixes: While it's tempting to seek immediate solutions to problems, focusing on long-term strategies and comprehensive solutions will be more effective in addressing the community's concerns. Negative community sentiment for a while will not make or break you, so breathe and find the right solution, not the quickest. Engaging in open dialogue with community members and seeking their input can help identify the root causes of issues and develop sustainable solutions.

3.   Avoid overpromising: Maintaining trust within the community is vital for successful community management. Be honest about your capabilities and resources, and communicate realistic expectations to avoid disappointment and resentment. Transparency in your actions and decisions will help foster a sense of trust and openness within the community.

4.   Don't ignore outliers: Inclusivity is a crucial aspect of effective community management. Ensure that you're giving attention to the unique concerns and perspectives of minority groups or individuals within the community. By doing so, you'll foster a sense of belonging and create an environment where everyone feels heard and valued. - But do not virtue act.

5.   Establish a Reporting Process: It's important to have a clear process for reporting and addressing incidents of harassment, hate speech, or other harmful behaviours. Ensure that community members know how to report incidents and that there is a system in place for promptly addressing and resolving these issues. This will help create a safe and supportive environment for everyone.

6.   Resist the urge to micromanage: Empower community members to take responsibility for their projects and contributions. Provide guidance and support when needed, but avoid excessive control over the community's development. This approach will foster a sense of ownership and commitment among community members, ultimately leading to a more dynamic and engaged community.

7.   Avoid over-reliance on metrics: While quantitative data can provide valuable insights into the effectiveness of your community management efforts, it's crucial to consider qualitative aspects as well. Engage with community members and gather feedback on their experiences, satisfaction levels, and sense of belonging. This information will help you better understand the overall health and well-being of the community.

8.   Don't dismiss negative feedback but also consider its representativeness: Negative feedback can provide valuable insights into areas of improvement for your community management efforts. Approach criticism with an open mind, but also consider its context and whether it accurately represents the majority's views. Strive to maintain a balanced perspective and use feedback as a tool for growth and improvement.

9.   Steer clear of unnecessary jargon: Effective communication is key to successful community management. Ensure that your messaging is clear, concise, and accessible to all community members. Avoid using technical terms or jargon that may alienate or confuse members, and always strive for inclusive language.

10.   Avoid one-size-fits-all solutions: Embrace the diversity within your community by recognizing that different members may have unique needs and preferences. Develop flexible solutions and offer multiple options or pathways to accommodate these diverse needs. This approach will contribute to a more inclusive and adaptable community environment.

11.   Cultural Sensitivity and Awareness: Being aware of cultural differences and demonstrating sensitivity towards them is essential for effective community management. Understand and respect the various cultural backgrounds, customs, and perspectives of your community members. This awareness will help create an inclusive environment where everyone feels welcome and valued.

Encouraging Engagement and Interaction in Online Communities

A thriving online community is characterised by high levels of engagement and interaction between its members.By leveraging psychological biases and creating opportunities for meaningful connections, community managers can foster an environment that keeps members actively participating and invested in the community. Here are several strategies for promoting engagement in online communities:

1. **Utilising Investment Bias**: Investment bias is the tendency for people to become more committed to something as they invest more time, effort, or resources into it. Encourage members to take on responsibilities or contribute their skills to the community, such as organising events, creating content, or mentoring new members. As members invest in the community, they are more likely to feel a sense of ownership and commitment to its success.

2. **Creating a Sense of Belonging**: Humans have a natural desire to belong and connect with others who share their interests and values. Develop a community identity by establishing shared goals, values, and a unique community culture. Encourage members to share their experiences, ideas, and personal stories, which can help create a sense of camaraderie and foster deeper connections.

3. **Incorporating Social Proof**: Social proof is the psychological phenomenon where people conform to the actions of others under the assumption that those actions are the correct behaviour. Highlight positive engagement and contributions from community members, such as featuring user-generated content, showcasing member accomplishments, or acknowledging outstanding participation. This can inspire others to follow suit and participate more actively in the community.

4. **Leveraging the Mere Exposure Effect**: The mere exposure effect is a psychological principle that suggests people tend to develop a preference for things they encounter frequently. Regularly share content and initiate discussions on relevant topics to keep the community active and familiar to its members. This will make members more comfortable engaging and interacting with one another.

5. **Facilitating Reciprocity**: Reciprocity is the natural inclination to return favours and respond in kind to positive actions. Encourage a culture of mutual support and assistance by prompting members to help one another, such as answering questions, sharing resources, or providing feedback on projects. When members experience the benefits of giving and receiving help, they are more likely to remain engaged and contribute to the community.

6. **Organising Collaborative Activities**: Create opportunities for members to work together on projects, challenges, or events that require collaboration and teamwork. By participating in group activities, members can forge stronger relationships and develop a greater sense of commitment to the community's success.

7. **Implementing Gamification**: Gamification involves applying game-like elements to non-game contexts to increase motivation and engagement. Introduce gamification elements such as leaderboards, points systems, or badges to reward active participation and acknowledge member accomplishments. This can tap into members' competitive nature and drive them to engage more actively in the community.

By understanding and leveraging human nature biases, community managers can create an engaging and interactive environment in online communities. By fostering a sense of belonging, providing opportunities for collaboration, and rewarding participation, community managers can encourage members to invest in the community and contribute to its growth and success.

Harnessing the Power of Engagement Campaigns

In this chapter, we delve into the concept of engagement campaigns as an influential strategy for community managers seeking to ignite interaction, disseminate crucial information, and inspire specific actions within their online communities.

We will examine innovative examples, such as treasure hunts and challenge-oriented initiatives, to demonstrate the effectiveness of these campaigns in fostering a sense of investment and dedication among community members while also addressing potential challenges and long-term implications.

The Benefits and Challenges of Engagement Campaigns

Engagement campaigns, including treasure hunts and challenge-driven activities, require community members to actively participate, solve problems, and complete tasks to progress through the campaign. These campaigns tap into the psychology of investment bias, where the more time and effort individuals devote to an activity, the more committed they become to its success.

Engagement campaigns offer several benefits:

Increased interaction: By creating a sense of challenge and competition, engagement campaigns encourage members to communicate, collaborate, and actively participate in the community.

Information dissemination: Treasure hunts and other challenge-based campaigns can be designed to guide participants through a path of hidden information or resources, effectively disseminating key messages and data.

Call to action: Engagement campaigns can trigger specific actions, such as signing up for a newsletter, joining a group, or participating in a project, by incorporating these tasks into the challenges.

Building camaraderie: Working together to solve problems and complete tasks fosters a sense of camaraderie and shared achievement among community members.

Enhanced community retention: The sense of investment and commitment generated by engagement campaigns can lead to increased community loyalty and long-term retention.

However, there are potential challenges to consider:

Resource constraints: Planning and executing engagement campaigns can be resource-intensive, requiring time, effort, and financial investments from community managers.

Managing expectations: Ensuring that participants' expectations are met while also maintaining a fair and transparent process can be challenging.

Balancing competition and collaboration: Encouraging a healthy balance between competition and collaboration among community members is essential to avoid potential conflicts.

The Mechanics of Engagement Campaigns with Practical Examples

Developing an effective engagement campaign requires careful planning and execution. Here are some key steps to consider, along with real-world examples for illustration:

Define objectives: Establish clear goals for the campaign, such as increasing interaction, disseminating information, or triggering a call to action. For example, a company might create an engagement campaign to promote a new product launch or drive sign-ups for an upcoming event.

Design challenges: Develop engaging, relevant, and appropriately difficult challenges that align with the campaign objectives and encourage participation. A coding community could design a series of coding challenges that require members to solve problems using specific programming languages or techniques.

Implement rewards: Offer incentives, such as exclusive content, access to special events, or even tangible prizes, to motivate participants and acknowledge their efforts. A gaming community might reward winners with in-game currency, merchandise, or access to exclusive content.

Monitor progress: Track participants' progress, provide guidance and support when necessary, and make adjustments to the campaign as needed to ensure its success. A fitness community could track the progress of participants in a weight loss challenge and offer support through coaching or group discussions.

Evaluate results: Assess the effectiveness of the campaign in achieving its objectives and gather feedback from participants to inform future campaigns. A book club might survey members after a reading challenge to gather feedback on the selection of books, the pacing of the challenge, and the overall experience.

Example 1: Treasure Hunt for a Blockchain Gaming Platform

A blockchain gaming platform organises a treasure hunt to increase user engagement and educate users about the platform's games and mechanics. The treasure hunt design considers human inclinations, such as the desire to satisfy curiosity, the appreciation for personal achievements, and the influence of peers, to create an engaging experience.

By creating a series of riddles or puzzles related to the in-game mechanics and the platform's token economy, the gaming platform ignites the participants' natural curiosity, encouraging them to explore and understand the game mechanics to solve the puzzles. This process of discovery taps into the innate human motivation to learn, known as the information gap theory.

The treasure hunt also fosters a stronger sense of ownership and attachment to the gaming ecosystem and its community by requiring participants to invest time and effort to find hidden tokens. This creates a greater appreciation for their discoveries, as they have personally contributed to achieving them, leveraging the endowment effect.

Finally, the platform can encourage participants to share their progress and achievements on social media, influencing other users to join the treasure hunt and engage with the platform. This approach utilises our natural tendency to be influenced by the behaviour and opinions of others, known as social proof.

Example 2: DeFi Platform's Educational Challenge Series

In this example, a decentralised finance (DeFi) platform aims to educate its community through a series of educational challenges that take into account human inclinations, such as the desire to see tasks through, the need for consistency, and the pride in self-accomplishment.

By designing a series of challenges with increasing difficulty, the DeFi platform encourages participants to continue engaging with the platform, driven by the desire to complete tasks they have already started and to make the most of the time and effort they have invested, tapping into the Zeigarnik effect.

To capitalise on the need for consistency, the platform can ask participants to publicly commit to completing the entire challenge series. Once committed, participants are more likely to follow through with their pledge, leading to increased engagement and learning, following the consistency principle.

Finally, the platform can require participants to interact with its tools and experiment with its features to complete the challenges, making users feel more invested in the DeFi ecosystem and its offerings. This hands-on experience allows users to take pride in their self-accomplishment and can lead to valuable feedback for the platform, contributing to its continuous improvement and growth.

Price Chat

In order to foster a healthy, supportive, and focused community, it is essential to maintain an environment that encourages meaningful discussions centred on the growth and development of the project. For this reason and more, price and market speculation discussions are not usually allowed in official groups. This policy is in place to ensure that the community remains focused on the project's core aspects, prevent market manipulation, maintain a professional atmosphere, and adhere to relevant regulations (particularly in relation to large exchanges such as Coinbase/Binance). By understanding and respecting these guidelines, community members can contribute to a thriving ecosystem that benefits everyone involved.

In the following section, we will delve deeper into the reasons behind this policy:

1) **Focus on Product and Community Development**: Our primary goal is to create a thriving community that supports and fosters the growth and development of the product or project. By restricting price talk, we maintain the focus on the core aspects of the project, such as technology, partnerships, and community engagement, rather than getting sidetracked by speculative price discussions.

2) **Prevent Market Manipulation**: Restricting price discussions helps to prevent the spread of misinformation, speculation, and potential market

manipulation. In open forums, it is difficult to verify the accuracy of statements made about price movements or IDOs, and such discussions can lead to individuals making uninformed decisions or engaging in harmful trading practices.

3) **Maintain a Professional Atmosphere**: By eliminating price talk, we aim to maintain a professional and respectful atmosphere in our community. This policy allows our community members to focus on constructive discussions that contribute to the growth and development of the project, rather than getting bogged down in heated debates over price movements or financial gains.

4) **Compliance with Regulations**: In some locales, discussing price movements or IDOs may be considered financial advice, and community managers or project leaders could potentially face legal consequences for allowing these discussions.Furthermore, large exchanges such as Coinbase may actively deny listings based on this one aspect. By restricting price talk, we ensure that we are in compliance with relevant regulations and minimise potential legal risks.

Example polite notice fyi -

Please respect our policy on restricted price talk and focus on fostering a positive and supportive environment that encourages meaningful discussions about [PROJECT]'s goals, technology, partnerships, and community development.

<u>Managing Conflicts and Disagreements</u>

<u>Poison apples - Dangers to the community</u>

As a community manager, one of your primary responsibilities is to cultivate a positive and welcoming environment for your members. While it may be tempting to focus solely on growing your community and bringing in as many members as possible, it is essential to also be aware of the potential negative impact that toxic individuals can have on your community.

These individuals, also known as "poison apples," can exhibit toxic behaviours that spread negativity and drive away other members, ultimately damaging your community's reputation. It's important to be proactive and vigilant in identifying toxic behaviour, regardless of the individual's popularity.

When identifying toxic behaviour, it is important to focus on the behaviour itself, rather than the individual. Just because someone is popular in other communities does not necessarily mean they will be a positive contributor to your community.

Look for patterns of toxic behaviour, such as excessive negativity, frequent arguing or fighting, or persistent personal attacks. Use analytics tools to monitor engagement rates and user feedback, which can help you identify problematic users.

Once you have identified a poison apple, it is essential to take swift and decisive action to remove them from the community. Depending on the severity of the situation, this may involve issuing warnings, temporary bans, or permanent account suspensions.

However, it is also essential to address the root causes of toxic behaviour. Sometimes, a toxic community member may be acting out of frustration or a sense of powerlessness. By addressing their underlying concerns, you may be able to turn a poison apple into a positive contributor to your community.

It is important to remember that some toxic individuals may have a following in other communities because they are seen as "truth seekers" or "contrarians" who challenge the status quo and question authority. While it's important to respect diverse opinions within your community, it's equally important to maintain a positive atmosphere.

By being proactive and vigilant in identifying toxic behaviour, and taking appropriate action, you can maintain a positive and welcoming environment for all members of your community. This will ultimately lead to a healthier, more engaged community that benefits everyone involved.

Respectful Dissent

Respectful dissent is an essential element of any healthy and functional community, but unfortunately, it can often be abused by those who seek to disrupt or undermine the community's values and objectives. Therefore, it's important to understand the risks and challenges associated with dissent, as well as the strategies that can help encourage respectful expression of opposing views.

One of the main risks of dissent is that it can easily escalate into personal attacks, harassment, and other forms of abusive behaviour. This can create a toxic environment that discourages participation and drives away members. Additionally, dissent can be used as a cover for hate speech, misinformation, and other harmful activities, which can pose a serious threat to the safety and well-being of community members.

To mitigate these risks and encourage respectful dissent, community area managers can work closely with their online community moderators to implement effective moderation policies and procedures. This includes establishing clear guidelines for acceptable behaviour, providing training and support to moderators, and promoting a culture of openness, tolerance, and respect.

Community area managers can also encourage respectful dissent by fostering an atmosphere of transparency and accountability. This means being open to feedback, addressing concerns promptly and fairly, and providing opportunities for members to voice their opinions and ideas. By creating a safe and supportive environment, community area managers can encourage members to express their views in a respectful and constructive manner, which can lead to positive change and growth.

In summary, respectful dissent is a crucial component of any thriving community, but it can also be fraught with risks and challenges. To promote a culture of respectful dissent, community area managers must work closely with their online community moderators to establish clear guidelines and procedures, foster a culture of openness and accountability, and provide training and support to moderators and members alike. By doing so, they can create a vibrant and inclusive community that is capable of navigating the complexities of dissent with grace and maturity.

Conflict Resolution

Conflicts are bound to arise in any community, and having a strategy to resolve them is crucial. When conflicts arise there are a number of key rules you need to follow:

I. **Actively listen** to all parties involved and seek to understand their perspectives (do not prepare an answer and simply wait for an opportunity to respond)

II. **Do not take commentary personally** no matter how personal it gets, the person is not angry at you, they do not know you. Remind yourself of this to <u>maintain a monotone response</u> without becoming patronising. It's a fine line but crucial.

III. **Control the tone.** If they get angry and you do not, their emotion will burn out. Only if you get worked up will they continue as such. <u>It is very hard to argue with a calm person</u>.

IV. **State your position firmly**. If you have a responsibility, state it clearly and own that position. Equally if you hold no responsibility, state that clearly.

V. **Do not give to receive** - If you try to resolve conflict by gifting in any form it will be abused, without question. Items received in this way will always result in a feeling of entitlement and what starts as a good will gesture results in poor optics all round, every time.

Along with these, consider employing specific conflict resolution techniques such as **mediation** or **structured dialogue** when addressing disputes within the community. These methods can facilitate constructive conversations and help parties reach mutually agreeable solutions. By using these techniques, community managers can effectively resolve conflicts while maintaining a positive atmosphere.

3

Identifying and Addressing Spammers and Scammers

<u>Identifying Stooges (Fake Users)</u>

In this section, we'll discuss how to identify stooges, or fake users, who work in tandem to promote a third-party app, product, or service. We'll cover the red flags to watch for, such as seemingly unrelated users suddenly discussing a specific topic or product, as well as techniques to verify the legitimacy of user accounts. Understanding how these deceptive tactics work will help you maintain a spam-free and secure online environment for your community.

Unusual Patterns of Activity: Keep an eye out for abnormal patterns of activity, such as a group of new users suddenly joining your platform and immediately discussing a particular topic or product. This can be a clear indication of coordinated efforts to promote a third-party app or service.

Sudden Topic or Product Promotion: If you notice a sudden surge in discussions or mentions of a specific product or service that is unrelated to your platform's usual content, this could be a sign of stooges promoting a third-party app.

Similar Usernames and Profile Information: Stooges often create multiple fake accounts with similar usernames or profile information. Look for patterns in usernames, profile pictures, and other account details that suggest a connection between seemingly unrelated users.

Generic or Scripted Comments: Fake users tend to use generic or scripted comments when promoting a product or service. Watch for repetitive language or identical phrases across multiple user accounts as this can be a sign of stooges at work.

Short Account Lifespan: Fake users often have a short account lifespan. Check the creation date of user accounts to identify potential stooges, as they may have been created recently for the sole purpose of promoting a third-party app or service.

Limited or No Engagement History: Stooges typically have limited or no engagement history with your platform, which can make them stand out from genuine users. Review user activity history to spot potential fake accounts.

Identifying Honey Traps

Honey traps refer to deceptive tactics that lure unsuspecting users into engaging with seemingly innocent or attractive offers, only to reveal hidden costs or consequences. Here are some examples of the most common types of honey trap.

The Attractive Persona Financial Scam

Scammers use attractive profile pictures and personas to manipulate emotions and persuade community members to provide financial assistance or investments. They often promise significant returns or share sob stories to appeal to the target's empathy. Exercise caution with such profiles and never send money to strangers online, regardless of their claims.

The Hidden Cost Offer

Scammers lure users with seemingly valuable items, cryptocurrencies, or digital assets, only to reveal hidden costs associated with receiving them. These costs may include transaction fees, taxes, or shipping charges. Scammers may also request personal information or wallet access. Be sceptical of any offers that seem too good to be true, especially from unverified sources.

The Fake Giveaway and Airdrop Scam

Scammers create fake giveaways or airdrops, promising free tokens or rewards in exchange for personal information, wallet access, or a small initial investment. Always verify the legitimacy of any giveaway or airdrop before participating and avoid sharing sensitive information with unverified sources.

The Seed Phrase Scammer Bait

Malicious actors may prey on individuals looking to take advantage of an unsuspecting victim by pretending to be uninformed about cryptocurrency and posting a wallet seed phrase. The wallet may contain tokens on a network like Ethereum, but with insufficient Ether to transfer them out. When someone attempts to steal the tokens by depositing Ether, the scammer takes control of the newly added Ether. These are unorthodox scams as they tend to prey on individuals willing to steal from another. So could strictly be seen as thieves stealing from thieves.

By educating community members about the risks associated with honey traps, you can contribute to a safer and more secure online community.

Identifying Paid FUDders

FUD (Fear, Uncertainty, and Doubt) refers to the spread of negative, misleading, and often false information aimed at undermining the confidence in a project, asset, or technology. Paid FUDders are individuals or groups who are financially compensated to create and disseminate FUD in order to manipulate market sentiment, usually for the benefit of their clients or themselves. Identifying paid FUDders can help maintain a healthy and informed community. Here are some tips to help you spot them:

Inconsistent Posting History
One way to identify potential paid FUDders is by examining their posting history. If an account has a history of consistently spreading negative information about various projects, or if their activity seems to coincide with market events or price fluctuations, they may be a paid FUDder.

Repetitive and Unsupported Claims
Paid FUDders often use repetitive and baseless claims to instil fear and uncertainty in the community. Look for individuals who repeatedly post negative statements without providing credible evidence or sources to back up their claims. Be sceptical of any claims that seem exaggerated or unfounded.

Manipulative Language and Tone
FUDders tend to use manipulative language and emotional appeals to influence the opinions of community members. They may employ scare

tactics, exaggerate risks, or use loaded phrases to create a sense of urgency or panic. Be cautious of individuals who consistently use such language in their posts or comments.

Coordinated Efforts

In some cases, paid FUDders may work together in a coordinated effort to spread misinformation more effectively. Look for patterns of similar language, claims, or timing among multiple accounts or posts. A coordinated FUD campaign may also involve multiple users upvoting or supporting each other's negative statements to increase their visibility.

To protect your community from the negative impact of paid FUDders, it is essential to stay vigilant and encourage a culture of critical thinking, open discussion, and fact-checking. By identifying and addressing FUD in a timely manner, you can maintain a healthy, well-informed, and engaged community.

Identifying Airdrop Hunters

Airdrop hunters are individuals who actively seek out and participate in airdrops, where free tokens or other rewards are distributed by blockchain projects, often as a promotional strategy. These individuals may join online communities primarily for the purpose of receiving airdrops, rather than genuinely engaging with the project or its community. While airdrop hunters are not always unwelcome, as they can contribute to the spread of information about a project, it is essential to identify them to maintain a balanced and engaged community. Here are some characteristics of airdrop hunters and tips on how to identify them:

Language and Phrasing

Airdrop hunters often use specific language in their posts or comments, frequently asking about or mentioning airdrops, giveaways, or free tokens. They might inquire about the distribution date, eligibility criteria, or the amount of tokens to be distributed. Keep an eye out for users who consistently use this language or focus solely on airdrops in their interactions.

Variation in Airdrop Hunters

Not all airdrop hunters are the same. Some may be genuinely interested in the project and participate in the community, while others may be solely motivated by the prospect of receiving free tokens. There are also those who use automated tools or scripts to join multiple communities and participate in airdrops simultaneously. Be aware of these variations when identifying airdrop hunters in your community.

Limited Engagement

Airdrop hunters may show limited engagement with the community beyond their interest in airdrops. They might not contribute to discussions about the project, its technology, or its development, and their participation may be limited to asking about or discussing airdrops. Monitor the engagement level of community members to identify potential airdrop hunters.

Account Activity

Accounts that join multiple communities, particularly those related to blockchain projects, may be a sign of an airdrop hunter. Reviewing the accounts they follow, the groups they belong to, or their posting history can provide clues about their motivations for joining your community.

Positive Impact

While it is essential to identify airdrop hunters, it is also important to recognize that they can have a positive impact on your community. They can help spread awareness about your project and increase its visibility, especially during promotional events or airdrops. Striking a balance between genuine community members and airdrop hunters can contribute to the growth and success of your project.

By identifying airdrop hunters and understanding their motivations, you can manage their presence in your community and maintain a healthy balance between engagement and promotional activities. Encourage genuine participation and foster a community that is genuinely interested in your project's success.

Identifying Malicious Paid Followers

Malicious paid followers are accounts, often bots, that are intentionally added to a community to inflate its follower count or create the appearance of fake engagement. These followers may be purchased by external parties with the intent to harm the project's reputation, implying that the project is engaging in dishonest promotional practices, or to potentially flood the community with spam or other unwanted content. Identifying and addressing malicious paid followers is crucial for maintaining the integrity of your community. Here are some tips to help you identify them:

Sudden Follower Growth
A sudden and unexpected increase in follower numbers without a corresponding increase in genuine engagement or activity within the community may indicate the presence of malicious paid followers. Monitor your community's growth and be vigilant for any unusual spikes in membership that cannot be explained by recent events or promotions.

Generic or Inauthentic Profiles

Malicious paid followers often have generic or inauthentic profiles, with limited personal information, stock profile photos, or a complete absence of a profile picture. These accounts may also have unusual usernames, which may consist of random characters or appear to be auto-generated. Review the profiles of new followers to identify potential fake accounts.

Lack of Engagement

Paid followers typically show little to no engagement with the community, as their primary purpose is to inflate the follower count. They rarely participate in discussions, post comments, or react to content shared by other members. Monitor the engagement level of community members and be cautious of accounts that show no signs of genuine participation.

Similarities Among Accounts

Malicious paid followers may share similarities in their account creation date, the communities they follow, or the content they post. Identifying patterns among multiple accounts can help you spot fake followers who have been added to your community for malicious purposes.

Spam or Unwanted Content

In some cases, malicious paid followers may flood the community with spam, phishing links, or other unwanted content. This could be an attempt to undermine the project's credibility, disrupt genuine discussions, or exploit community members. Keep an eye out for any sudden increases in spam or suspicious content within your community.

Implementing Anti-Spam Measures and Tools

Effective anti-spam measures and tools are essential for maintaining a healthy, engaged, and spam-free online community. By proactively implementing these measures, you can minimise the impact of spam, unwanted content, and malicious activity within your community. Here are some recommended tools and strategies for Discord and Telegram:

Discord Servers:

Mee6: *Mee6 is a versatile and customizable bot that offers a range of features, including **AI moderation**, a **ticketing system**, and an If This Then That **(IFTTT) system**. Use Mee6 to set up automated **moderation rules** to **prevent spam**, filter out **unwanted content**, and **enforce community guidelines**. The bot can also be configured to re**ward active users**, **manage roles**, and provide **helpful information** to community members*

Telegram:

Group Help Bot: The Group Help Bot (https://t.me/GroupHelpBot) is a powerful and customizable moderation tool for Telegram communities. Configure the bot using the BotFather (https://t.me/BotFather) to establish anti-spam rules, set up automated moderation, and enforce community guidelines. The Group Help Bot can also assist in managing group permissions, roles, and other administrative tasks.

Group Staff Bot: The Group Staff Bot (https://t.me/ghStaffBot) works in tandem with the Group Help Bot to identify administrators without requiring them to use monikers. This enables admins to maintain a lower profile while still being able to perform moderation tasks effectively.

Telegram Translator Bot: The Telegram Translator Bot (https://t.me/TgTranslatorBot) is a helpful tool for on-the-fly translation within your community. This can be particularly useful in international communities where language barriers may impede communication and engagement. The Translator Bot can help bridge those gaps and create a more inclusive and accessible environment for all members.

In addition to these tools, consider implementing the following general anti-spam measures in your community:

1) Set clear community guidelines and expectations regarding spam and unwanted content. Make these guidelines easily accessible to all members.

2) Require new members to complete a verification process, such as completing a CAPTCHA or confirming their email address, to prevent automated bots from joining the community.

3) Monitor community activity and engagement regularly, and take prompt action to address spam or malicious activity as needed.

4) Encourage community members to report spam or suspicious activity to moderators or administrators.

Implementing these anti-spam measures and tools, will help you maintain a safe, engaged, and spam-free environment for your community members.

4

Measurement and Evaluation

Measurement and Evaluation

Effectively measuring and evaluating your community management efforts is crucial for understanding the impact of your strategies, identifying areas for improvement, and fostering a thriving community. Combining quantitative and qualitative data helps gain a comprehensive understanding of your community's health and informs decision-making. Here's a structured approach to measure and evaluate your community's success:

I. Quantitative Metrics

A. Key Metrics to Measure

Engagement: Monitor the level of activity, such as posts, comments, reactions, and shares. Observe changes in engagement over time to identify trends and assess the effectiveness of your community management strategies.

Retention: Evaluate the rate at which members remain active in your community over time. High retention rates indicate a positive community experience and successful management practices.

Growth: Track the rate of community growth, including new members, followers, or subscribers. Steady growth signifies effective promotional efforts and a healthy community.

Conversion: Measure the rate of community members taking desired actions, such as signing up for a newsletter, making a purchase, or attending an event. Higher conversion rates indicate effective community management strategies driving tangible results.

B. Implementing Quantitative Measurements

Analytics Tools: Utilise platform-provided analytics tools (e.g., Discord Server Insights, Telegram Analytics, or Facebook Group Insights) to monitor engagement, retention, growth, and conversion rates. Export data to a spreadsheet or data visualisation tool for trend and pattern analysis.

Custom Tracking: Implement custom tracking solutions like UTM tags for shared links or event tracking for specific actions to measure campaign and initiative effectiveness.

Regular Reports: Generate regular reports (weekly, monthly, or quarterly) to analyse data over time, identify trends, and assess the impact of community management strategies.

II. Qualitative Measures

A. Key Metrics to Measure

Member Satisfaction: Assess community members' satisfaction with the community experience, including content quality, moderator responsiveness, and the overall atmosphere.

Focus Groups: Gather in-depth insights into community members' experiences, needs, and expectations through focus groups or roundtable discussions.

One-on-One Conversations: Engage in one-on-one conversations with community members to understand individual perspectives and experiences.

Anecdotal Feedback: Encourage community members to share their thoughts, opinions, and experiences openly, either through dedicated feedback channels or during community events.

B. Implementing Qualitative Measurements

Surveys and Polls: Use tools like Google Forms, SurveyMonkey, or Typeform to create and distribute surveys or polls for collecting community feedback.

Focus Groups: Organise virtual or in-person focus group sessions with a diverse selection of community members. Use video conferencing tools (e.g., Zoom, Google Meet) or arrange physical meetups, if possible. Prepare a list of questions or discussion topics in advance.

One-on-One Conversations: Schedule one-on-one conversations with community members through direct messages or video calls. Utilise tools like Calendly for scheduling and leverage built-in messaging and calling features on your community platform.

Feedback Channels: Establish dedicated feedback channels within your community, such as specific threads, chat rooms, or forms, for members to share thoughts, opinions, and experiences. Monitor these channels regularly and document feedback.

III. Continuous Improvement Process

1. **Data Compilation**:

   Organise and compile the quantitative and qualitative data gathered into a single document, spreadsheet, or data visualisation tool.

2. **Data Analysis**:

   Analyse the data to identify trends, patterns, and areas for improvement. Look for correlations between quantitative metrics and qualitative feedback to deepen your understanding of community health.

3. **Action Plan**:

   Develop an action plan addressing identified areas for improvement, such as revising content strategies, enhancing moderation practices, or implementing new tools and resources to better support community members.

4. **Implementation and Monitoring**:

   Implement the changes outlined in your action plan and continue to monitor your community's performance through regular data collection and analysis. Adjust your strategies as needed based on the data and feedback collected. By consistently measuring and evaluating your community's success, you can ensure that your efforts remain aligned with the needs and expectations of your members, fostering a thriving, engaged community.

5

Developing a Community Growth
Strategy

Leveraging Social Media and Online Channels

In today's digital age, social media and online channels are the go-to tools for building and nurturing communities of all kinds. Whether you're a brand, a nonprofit, a hobbyist, or anything in between, social media and online channels offer unparalleled opportunities to connect with like-minded folks, build relationships, and expand your reach.

But let's be real. Social media and online channels aren't all sunshine and rainbows. They come with their fair share of challenges and pitfalls that can trip you up if you're not careful. *Fragmented conversations*, *trolls*, *spam*, and *privacy breaches*, as covered in earlier sections, are just a few of the hazards that can derail your community management efforts. So, how do you navigate these choppy waters and emerge victorious on the other side?

That's where this section comes in. Below are some of the key benefits and potential pitfalls of using social media and online channels for community management. We'll also give you practical advice on how to leverage these platforms effectively, such as choosing the most relevant platforms, setting clear objectives, and developing a content strategy.

Benefits:

- ✔ **Increased visibility and reach**: Utilising various social media and online channels can significantly expand your community's visibility and help attract new members.
- ✔ **Networking opportunities**: Social media and online channels facilitate connections with like-minded individuals and organisations, fostering collaboration and partnerships.
- ✔ **Real-time communication**: Instant messaging and notifications enable rapid information exchange, promoting timely discussions and problem-solving.
- ✔ **User-generated content**: Community members can create and share content, leading to a diverse range of perspectives and experiences
- ✔ **Cost-effective marketing**: Social media and online channels provide a cost-effective way to promote your community and its events, products, or services.

Potential Pitfalls:

- X **Fragmentation**: Presence on multiple platforms can result in fragmented conversations and reduced engagement if not managed properly.
- X **Trolls and spam**: Online platforms are prone to spam and trolls, which can negatively impact your community if left unchecked.
- X **Time and resource-intensive**: Managing multiple platforms and creating content requires a significant time investment and may strain your team's resources.
- X **Reputation management**: Negative comments, reviews, or interactions on social media can harm your community's reputation if not addressed promptly and **effectively.**
- X **Overemphasis on self-promotion**: Excessive promotion of your community or its offerings may deter potential members or disengage current ones.
- X **Inauthenticity**: Automated posting, excessive use of buzzwords, or insincere engagement can diminish your community's credibility and trustworthiness.
- X **Privacy and security concerns**: Sharing personal information on social media platforms can expose community members to potential privacy breaches or cyberattacks.
- X **Algorithm changes**: Social media platforms frequently update their algorithms, which may affect your content's visibility and reach.

Practical Pointers:

1. **Focus on the most relevant platforms**: Choose social media and online channels that are popular among your target audience, such as *Twitter, Reddit, Telegram, Discord*, and *LinkedIn*. Avoid spreading yourself too thin across too many platforms.
2. **Establish clear objectives**: Set specific goals for each platform, such as increasing engagement, driving traffic to your website, or attracting new members.
3. **Develop a content strategy**: Plan and schedule your content to maintain a consistent posting frequency, including a mix of informative, engaging, and promotional content.
4. **Encourage cross-platform engagement**: Share content across platforms and promote your other channels to increase visibility and engagement.
5. **Collaborate with relevant influencers and communities:** Partner with thought leaders, influencers, and other communities within your niche or industry to expand your reach, credibility, and visibility. Collaborate on content or events that showcase your mutual interests.
6. **Measure and analyse your results**: Track platform-specific metrics to evaluate the effectiveness of your strategies and adjust as needed. Use tools like Google Analytics, platform-specific analytics, and social media management tools to monitor your progress. Regularly assess key performance indicators (KPIs) such as engagement, reach, and conversions to fine-tune your approach.

7. **Maintain a consistent brand identity**: Ensure that your branding, tone, and messaging are consistent across all platforms to reinforce your community's identity and create a cohesive experience for your audience.

8. **Prioritise community interaction**: Actively engage with your community members by responding to comments, asking questions, and participating in discussions. Authentic and consistent interaction helps foster trust and loyalty among community members.

Leveraging social media and online channels effectively can help you grow and engage your community.

Carefully considering the benefits and potential dangers, and implementing practical advice, you can maximise the impact of these platforms. As your community evolves, remember to continually refine your strategies to address changing needs and preferences. Staying agile and responsive will ensure long-term success in community management.

Hosting Events, Contests, and Giveaways

Organising events, contests, and giveaways can be a highly effective way to engage your community, encourage interaction, and attract new members. These initiatives not only provide value to your community but also help strengthen relationships and foster a sense of belonging. When planning and executing these activities, consider the insights gained from your measurement and evaluation efforts, as well as the unique needs and preferences of your community members.

Events

Events are gatherings, either online or in-person, where community members come together to learn, discuss, or network. Examples include Twitter Spaces, live events, AMA (Ask Me Anything) sessions on Reddit or Discord, and product demonstrations.

Pros:

- *Boost engagement and interaction among community members.*
- *Strengthen relationships within the community.*
- *Provide opportunities for members to learn and grow.*
- *Increase awareness and visibility of your project.*
- *Offer a platform for the project team to address questions and concerns.*

Cons:

- *Can require significant time and resources to plan and execute.*
- *May have limited reach, depending on the platform used.*
- *Engagement may be dependent on the event's topic and format.*
- *Scheduling can be challenging due to time zone differences.*

Example Campaign: AMA with the Project Team

1. *Set a date, time, and platform for the AMA (e.g., Discord or Reddit).*
2. *Prepare a list of topics and questions to be covered during the AMA.*
3. *Create promotional materials, such as banners or social media graphics, to announce the AMA.*
4. *Promote the AMA on all community channels (Twitter, Telegram, Discord) and encourage members to share the event with their networks.*
5. *Prepare the project team for the AMA by providing them with a list of potential questions and talking points.*
6. *Host the AMA and encourage community members to participate and ask questions.*
7. *After the event, compile a summary of the AMA, including key highlights and takeaways, and share it with the community.*
8. *Evaluate the success of the AMA by measuring engagement, attendance, and feedback from community members.*

Contests

Contests are competitive activities where community members can showcase their skills, creativity, or knowledge to win prizes. Examples include design competitions, trivia quizzes, and prediction contests.

Pros:

- *Encourage creativity and participation from community members.*
- *Generate user-generated content, such as designs or testimonials.*
- *Attract new members interested in the contest theme or prizes.*
- *Increase brand exposure and visibility.*
- *Offer opportunities to identify and reward top contributors.*

Cons:

- *Can be time-consuming to plan, promote, and manage.*
- *Requires resources for prizes and promotions.*
- *May attract participants who are only interested in winning prizes.*
- *Judging process can be subjective and may cause disagreements.*
- *Results may not align with the community's expectations or preferences.*

Example Campaign: Design a New Community Logo Contest

1. *Define the contest's objective, timeline, and rules.*
2. *Determine the prizes for the contest winners.*

3. Create promotional materials, such as banners or social media graphics, to announce the contest.
4. Promote the contest on all community channels (Twitter, Telegram, Discord) and encourage members to participate.
5. Provide clear guidelines and submission instructions for participants.
6. Monitor and collect submissions throughout the contest period.
7. Assemble a judging panel to review the submissions and select the winners based on predefined criteria.
8. Announce the contest winners and distribute the prizes accordingly.
9. Share the winning designs with the community and incorporate them into the community's branding.
10. Evaluate the contest's success by measuring engagement, submissions, and feedback from community members.

Giveaways

Giveaways are promotional activities where community members can win prizes through a random selection process. They differ from contests in that winners are chosen by chance, rather than based on skill, creativity, or knowledge. Examples include token airdrops, raffles, and social media sweepstakes.

Pros:

- Easy to set up and execute, with minimal time and resources required.
- Encourage community members to participate and engage with your content.
- Attract new members interested in the giveaway prizes.
- Boost brand exposure and visibility.
- Foster a sense of excitement and anticipation within the community.

Cons:

- May attract participants who are only interested in winning prizes.
- The value of prizes can affect the level of engagement and participation.
- May require compliance with legal regulations and platform guidelines.
- Lacks the opportunity to showcase skill or creativity, unlike contests.

- Results may not lead to long-term engagement or retention of new members.

Example Campaign: Social Media Sweepstakes Giveaway

1. *Define the giveaway's objective, timeline, and rules.*
2. *Determine the prizes for the giveaway winners.*
3. *Create promotional materials, such as banners or social media graphics, to announce the giveaway.*
4. *Promote the giveaway on all community channels (Twitter, Telegram, Discord) and encourage members to participate.*
5. *Provide clear guidelines and entry instructions for participants, such as following your social media accounts, liking and sharing a specific post, or tagging friends.*
6. *Monitor and collect entries throughout the giveaway period.*
7. *Use a random selection tool to choose the winners from the pool of participants.*
8. *Announce the giveaway winners and distribute the prizes accordingly.*
9. *Share the winners' names or usernames with the community to celebrate their success.*
10. *Evaluate the giveaway's success by measuring engagement, entries, and feedback from community members.*

By carefully considering the pros and cons of each option, as well as their specific requirements and benefits, you can select the most suitable type of event, contest, or giveaway for your community. Always remember to plan and execute these activities with your community's goals and interests in mind, as this will help ensure their success and contribute to the overall growth and engagement of your community.

6

Conclusion

Adapting to Changing Community Needs and Trends

The dynamic nature of the blockchain sector necessitates continuous adaptation and responsiveness from community managers to ensure their communities remain relevant, engaging, and valuable. By staying informed of industry trends, technological advancements, and evolving user preferences, community managers can effectively address the ever-changing needs and expectations of their members. Here are some key strategies for adapting to these changes:

Staying up-to-date with industry developments: Regularly monitoring industry news, attending conferences, webinars, or workshops, and engaging in relevant online forums can help community managers stay informed of the latest trends and advancements in the blockchain sector. This knowledge enables them to introduce new topics of discussion, offer valuable resources, and keep members informed and engaged.

Conducting regular community audits: Community managers should periodically assess the community's current state, including its demographics, interests, needs, and preferences. This can be done through surveys, feedback sessions, or analysing user behaviour and engagement patterns. By understanding the community's current needs, community managers can better tailor their strategies and initiatives to match these requirements.

Implementing feedback loops: Encouraging and incorporating member feedback is crucial for fostering a sense of ownership and investment in the community. By regularly soliciting feedback and acting on it, community managers demonstrate their commitment to meeting member needs, which in turn helps to maintain engagement and satisfaction.

Experimenting with new formats and platforms: As technology evolves, community managers should be open to exploring new communication channels, formats, or platforms that might better cater to the needs of their members. This can include adopting new social media platforms, integrating chatbots for customer support, or experimenting with virtual or augmented reality experiences.

Encouraging innovation and collaboration: Fostering a culture of innovation and collaboration within the community can help drive its growth and success. By empowering members to propose and execute new ideas, community managers can create an environment where creativity thrives and members feel invested in the community's future.

Adjusting community guidelines and policies: As the community evolves, it may be necessary to update or modify community guidelines and policies to better reflect its current needs and objectives. Community managers should be transparent and communicative about any changes, ensuring that members understand the rationale behind them and how they will benefit the community as a whole.

In conclusion, the ongoing role of community management in the blockchain sector involves staying attuned to the ever-changing landscape, adapting to the evolving needs of members, and continually striving to create an engaging and valuable community experience. By employing the strategies discussed above, community managers can ensure their communities remain relevant, successful, and purpose-driven, while fostering a sense of trust, collaboration, and investment among their members.

Final Thoughts

To close out *The Community Builders Handbook*, let us summarise, effective community management is critical for building and maintaining strong relationships with customers and stakeholders. Throughout this handbook, we've explored various strategies and techniques that can help you create a vibrant and engaged community. By establishing a shared purpose, spotlighting success stories, setting community guidelines, encouraging engagement and interaction, managing conflicts, identifying and addressing spammers and scammers, measuring and evaluating the community's effectiveness, developing a growth strategy, and hosting events, contests, and giveaways, you can build and maintain a thriving community that supports your organisation's goals and helps create lasting relationships with your customers and stakeholders.

It's important to note that community management is an ongoing process that requires dedication, patience, and a willingness to adapt to changing circumstances. By consistently implementing these strategies and techniques and regularly evaluating their effectiveness, you can continue to improve and grow your community. Remember to always keep your members at the centre of your efforts and strive to create a positive and supportive environment that encourages participation and engagement.

Thank you for taking the time to read this handbook. We hope that the insights and strategies presented here will be useful in building and maintaining a thriving community for your organisation. Good luck!

7

Glossary of Community Management Terms

General Community Management

- **Active Engagement**: The consistent and meaningful participation of community members in discussions, activities, and events.
- **Ambassador Program**: A strategy implemented by community managers to identify and engage with influential or highly active members, who can help promote the community, its values, and its content.
- **Asynchronous Communication**: Communication within a community that occurs without the need for participants to be online simultaneously, allowing for flexibility and convenience in discussions.
- **Ban**: The act of permanently removing a user from a community, typically as a consequence of severe or repeated violations of community guidelines.
- **Closed Community**: A type of community that requires an invitation, approval, or membership to access and participate in discussions and activities.
- **Community Health**: A measure of the overall well-being and functioning of a community, including factors such as member engagement, satisfaction, and adherence to community guidelines.
- **Community Onboarding**: The process of welcoming and integrating new members into a community, ensuring they understand the community's purpose, guidelines, and expectations.
- **Community Retention**: Strategies employed by community managers to maintain and increase member satisfaction and engagement, encouraging members to remain active and committed to the community.
- **Cross-Promotion**: A collaborative effort between communities or community managers to promote each other's content, events, or initiatives, often for mutual benefit and growth.

- **Digital Etiquette**: The set of behaviours and norms expected of community members when interacting in an online environment, promoting respectful and productive communication.
- **Feedback Loop**: A process that involves collecting and analysing feedback from community members, using the insights to make improvements, and communicating the changes back to the community.
- **Icebreakers**: Activities or prompts designed to facilitate introductions, build connections, and encourage interaction among community members, particularly during online events or in new community spaces.
- **Inclusive Language**: Language that is respectful and considerate of diverse backgrounds, experiences, and identities, promoting a sense of belonging and inclusivity within a community.
- **Muting**: The act of temporarily or permanently disabling a user's ability to communicate within a community, often as a consequence of violating community guidelines or exhibiting disruptive behaviour.
- **Open Community**: A type of community that allows anyone to join and participate without restrictions or barriers.
- **Online Reputation Management**: Strategies and practices employed by community managers to monitor, address, and influence the online perception of their community, its members, or its associated brand.
- **Safe Space**: An environment where community members feel comfortable and supported in expressing their thoughts, feelings, and experiences without fear of judgement, ridicule, or harassment.
- **Social Listening**: The process of monitoring and analysing online conversations, trends, and sentiments to better understand the community's interests, concerns, and preferences.
- **Synchronous Communication**: Communication within a community that occurs in real-time, such as live chats or video calls, fostering immediacy and presence in discussions.

- **Time Zone Sensitivity**: The consideration and awareness of time zone differences among community members when scheduling events, meetings, or activities, ensuring inclusivity and accessibility for all.
- **Trolls**: Individuals who engage in disruptive or provocative behaviour within a community, often with the intention of inciting conflict, anger, or negative reactions from other members.

Conflict Management and Moderation

- **Content Moderation**: The process of reviewing, filtering, and managing user-generated content within a community to ensure compliance with community guidelines and maintain a positive environment.
- **Conflict Resolution**: The process of addressing and resolving disagreements or disputes between community members through open communication, empathy, and compromise.
- **Poison Apples**: Toxic community members who exhibit disruptive or harmful behaviour, often causing conflicts or negatively impacting the community's atmosphere.
- **Respectful Dissent**: The act of expressing disagreement or differing opinions within a community in a constructive and respectful manner, fostering open and healthy discussions.

Engagement Strategies and Metrics

- **Community Metrics**: Quantitative and qualitative measurements used to evaluate the success, health, and growth of a community, including factors such as engagement levels, member satisfaction, and retention rates.

- **Gamification**: The incorporation of game-like elements and mechanics into community activities and interactions, designed to increase member engagement, motivation, and satisfaction.
- **Virtual Events**: Online gatherings, such as webinars, workshops, or meetups, that bring community members together to learn, collaborate, or socialise.

Security and Fraud Detection

- **Anti-Spam Measures**: Tools and strategies implemented by community managers to identify, prevent, and address unwanted or repetitive content, such as spam messages, advertisements, or links.
- **Honey Trap**: A deceptive tactic used by scammers or malicious actors, often involving the creation of fake profiles or the promise of rewards, to lure unsuspecting community members into revealing sensitive information or making unwise decisions.
- **Stooges**: False or misleading user profiles, created for the purpose of spreading misinformation, promoting scams, or manipulating community discussions.

Common Community Slang and Jargon

- **Degen**: A term used to describe someone who takes high risks in cryptocurrency trading or investments, often with a reckless disregard for potential losses.

- **FOMO (Fear of Missing Out)**: The feeling of anxiety or concern that one might miss out on an opportunity or trend, often leading to impulsive decision-making.
- **GM (Good Morning)**: A friendly greeting used in online communities, particularly in chat platforms like Telegram and Discord.
- **HODL**: A misspelling of "hold" that has become a popular term in the cryptocurrency community, encouraging users to hold onto their investments rather than selling them during periods of market volatility.
- **Moon/Mooning**: A term used to describe the rapid increase in the value of a cryptocurrency, often due to hype or a positive market trend.
- **Rug Pull**: A type of scam in which project creators suddenly withdraw funds or liquidity from a project, causing a rapid collapse in its value and leaving investors with significant losses.
- **Ser (Sir)**: A friendly term of address or salutation used in online communities, particularly in chat platforms like Telegram and Discord.
- **Fren (Friend)**: An informal term used to refer to friends or acquaintances within an online community.
- **Whale**: An individual or entity that holds a large amount of a particular cryptocurrency, often with the ability to influence market trends due to their significant holdings.
- **DYOR (Do Your Own Research)**: A reminder for individuals to conduct independent research and analysis before making investment decisions or participating in a project.